Paint Your Pet

METRO BOOKS
NEW YORK

By Patricia Getha, Marilyn Grame, Eileen Sorg, and Nolon Stacey

Tools & Materials

Drawing Materials

From quality graphite pencils to drawing paper, this kit includes all the materials you'll need to begin drawing your favorite pets right away. It's a good idea to get familiar with your tools before beginning the projects, so experiment as you read the information below.

Eraser

Use the rubber eraser to make adjustments, correct mistakes, or pull out highlights. You also may want a kneaded eraser that can be molded into different shapes and dabbed at areas to remove tone.

Sharpener

Use the hand-held sharpener in this kit to give your pencils sharp tips. A fine point can be used to create extremely thin lines and small details. You also can use the side of a sharp tip to quickly shade large areas with thick pencil strokes.

Graphite Pencil

Pencils with soft leads (labeled B for "black") make dense, dark marks, and the hard leads (labeled H for "hard") produce fine, light gray lines. This kit includes H and 2B pencils, but you may want to purchase additional pencils with varying lead grades.

Charcoal Pencil

You also may want to get a charcoal pencil. Made from packed, charred wood, charcoal is very soft and leaves a rich, black mark that blends and smudges easily.

Colored Pencils

You also may want to use colored pencils to render your animal portraits. Colored pencils are brightly hued and precise tools that are simple to use.

Setting Up Your Workspace

You don't need a professional drafting table to start drawing—many brilliant drawings have been created on a kitchen table! You'll need a hard surface to use as a drawing board, and something to prop up the board with, such as a stack of books. Good lighting is essential—it's best to work in natural light, but you also can purchase a daylight bulb, which gives off good white light. Make sure there are no shadows falling across your work area and use a comfortable chair with proper back support.

Painting Materials

One of the best aspects of watercolor painting is that a fine painting can be accomplished with a minimum amount of equipment. This kit contains all the necessary tools and materials for getting started on your pet portraits in watercolor.

Paints

The colors in this kit are burnt sienna, crimson red, ivory black, lemon yellow, permanent green, ultramarine blue, and yellow ochre. You also may want to buy Chinese white or white gouache.

Paint Brushes

This kit includes a flat brush for covering large areas and applying washes, as well as a round brush with a tapered point for a variety of paint strokes and fine details.

Paint Palette

The palette contains wells for pooling and mixing colors while painting. The plastic easily wipes clean and can be re-used again and again.

Extras

Keep a jar of water nearby to rinse brushes. A toothbrush, alcohol, paper towels, and a sponge each can be used to create special effects. A spray bottle will help keep your paints moist and a hair dryer can reduce drying time.

Drawing Techniques

Gradating and Blending

You can create a shaded gradation (from light to dark or dark to light) by switching to a harder or softer pencil, respectively, or by gradually changing the pressure applied on the pencil. The harder you press, the darker the stroke will be. By creating scales like those shown at right, you can see the range of *values* (the relative lightness or darkness of black) that various pressure amounts and pencil grades produce. Blend your scale for a smoother gradation. Blending is particularly useful when you want even tones or subtle pencil strokes, and can be used to create many textures. You can blend with tortillons, that come in a variety of sizes, or with a tissue.

Value Scale: Changing Pencils

This gradation of value begins with a 5B pencil, merges into a 5H, and finally ends with the white of the paper.

Value Scale: Smoothing the Tones

For a seamless gradation, blend the tones with a tissue.

Building Form and Creating Textures

Using a Tortillon

Tortillons can create lines over a large area, as shown, or smooth out tight areas.

Creating Form with Shading

By using darker values as you move away from the light source, you can give a sphere the appearance of form and depth. On the right sphere, the lines follow the contour of the curve; the darker and denser texture in the shadow areas communicate its form.

Drawing Hair with an Eraser

To create hair texture, apply a solid layer of shading. Then use an eraser tip to pull out short lines in the direction of hair growth.

Using Negative Drawing for Hair

Negative drawing means defining an object by filling in the area around it rather than the object itself. This method is great for drawing hair. Once the negative space is shaded, you can add texture and tone to individual hairs to give them more realism and depth.

Painting Techniques

Color Basics

Some basic knowledge about color will go a long way when it comes to mixing your own paints. The *primary colors* (red, yellow, and blue) are the three basic colors that can't be created by mixing other colors. All other colors are derived from these three. Each combination of two primaries results in a *secondary color* (purple, green, or orange), and a combination of a primary color and a secondary color results in a *tertiary color* (such as red-orange or red-purple). On the color wheel, at right, the colors across from each other are complementary colors, and groups of adjacent colors are *analogous* colors.

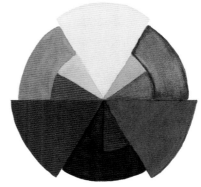

Color Wheel

A color wheel demonstrates color relationships. Knowing how colors relate to one another will help you create different moods.

Special Techniques and Effects

Flat Wash

For large areas of solid color, load the flat brush and create sweeping horizontal strokes that overlap for a seamless blend.

Graded Wash

Apply color as you would a flat wash, but add more water with each successive stroke to graduate color from dark to light.

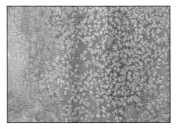

Using Salt

Sprinkle salt over wet paint; then brush it away when dry to create a dappled texture.

Scraping

Use a pointed tool, such as a brush handle, to scrape away wet paint, revealing lighter values beneath.

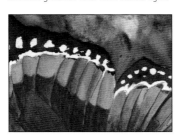

Wet-into-Wet

Paint wet color onto a wet support to produce soft edges and smooth blends.

Wet-into-Dry

Paint wet color onto a dry surface for crisper edges and more control over the spread of color.

Labrador Retriever

with Nolon Stacey

Step One

Step One

As I want this drawing to be a very detailed and lifelike portrait, I use the grid method to create my line drawing. (See steps one, two, and three on page 20.) Once I have my detailed outline in place, I immediately dive into detailed shading. Using a 2B pencil, I apply tone in the darkest areas: the pupils, the skin surrounding the eyes, the edges of nostrils, and the mouth area. I move on to the nose using an HB pencil, drawing very small circles and varying the size and pressure to suggest the form. I am careful to leave the tops and sides of the nose white where the light is reflecting. In this case, the insides of the nostrils aren't black—the light is reflecting within.

Step Two

To complete the nose, I use an HB pencil to apply a layer of slightly larger circles over the entire nose, toning down the highlights and adding texture. I also apply dark shading below the nose with a 2B pencil. As I move outward, I draw short lines that converge to a point, suggesting gaps between the light hairs. Before addressing the mouth's interior, I indent whiskers and hairs along the upper lip. Then I use the 2B pencil to add tone to the gums, giving them a smooth and moist look by leaving small specks of white. Now I shade the tongue with an HB pencil. I use this shadow to suggest its form, curving the shadow over the tongue's surface.

Step Three

I now begin to work on the fur. A Labrador has a short, yellow coat, so I will render it almost exclusively using a sharp HB pencil and short strokes that follow the direction of hair growth. I leave quite a lot of white paper showing through my lines to keep the fur light. To change the tone, I simply apply the lines closer together or farther apart to create darker or lighter areas. To make the rest of the head a little less daunting, I look for darker areas of fur, such as around the ears, and shade these first. This breaks up the space and creates smaller areas to work on.

Step Four

From the muzzle, I continue up and over the top of the head with the HB, taking the hair back and out toward the ears. I leave the bridge of the muzzle and the area above the eyes almost completely white, as this is where the light is hitting the dog's head directly. I apply very few light lines with a 2H pencil to indicate some hair here.

Step Five

I work on the ears in two stages. In stage one, I create the texture of the ears using an HB pencil. I make a ridge at the inner edge of the ear where it folds slightly. I curve my lines around the edges of the ear, giving the impression that the coat continues on the other side. The light on the left ear is strong, so I leave it almost completely white.

Step Six

In stage two, I simply apply an even layer of HB pencil over the ears, making sure that I don't apply too much pressure—I don't want this layer to be as dark as the lines I laid in the first stage. A Labrador's ears are generally darker than its body, so I also blend the area with a tissue until I reach the desired shade. I use the same two-stage method (laying in lines with an HB pencil, then shading over the top) for the area directly below the mouth.

Step Seven

Now I work on the collar. There are just two textures here to re-create—the fabric band and the buckle. First I indent strands of hair over the band to protect them from tone. Then I lay down ridges along the band using parallel lines and a 2B pencil. To give the ridges form, I lightly shade to the left of each line. I finish the band by applying a layer of HB pencil over it. The metal buckle is slightly more intricate. I add the sharp edges with a 2B pencil and shade over the entire area with an H pencil. I lift out highlights with a kneaded eraser. You can see that I have extended the highlight slightly beyond the actual buckle—this makes it appear to really shine. Once I finish the buckle, I create the coat below the neck. First I add a layer of H pencil, blending the strokes with a tissue. Then I go over the area with an HB pencil, stroking in the directions of hair growth. To keep the viewer's focus on the head, I fade out gradually along the bottom for a soft, subtle edge.

Fish in Bowl

with Eileen Sorg

Step 1

I begin by sketching the basic outline of the subject, and then I trace the image onto tracing paper. Next I coat the underside of the tracing paper with an even layer of graphite or place transfer paper between my sketch and a sheet of drawing paper. I use very light lines to transfer the basic outline onto the drawing paper.

Step 2

Now I pull out my colored pencils and use cool gray 30% to outline the shape of the fishbowl and shade areas of the goldfish. Then I add darker outlines to the bowl using warm gray 50%. I bring in some light cerulean blue for the water. Next I add slate gray to the bottom of the bowl and along the surface of the water.

Step 3

I lighten the outlines of the fish with an eraser; then I fill them in with deco yellow. I apply lavender over the gray areas on the fish.

Step 4

I cover the majority of both fish with pale vermilion, leaving some of the lavender showing through. Then I use black to fill in the pupils and create the gill on the fish on the right.

Step 5

I create the mouths with black. Then I accent the fish with the scarlet lake colored pencil and erase any remaining pencil lines.

 *Parrot*

with Eileen Sorg

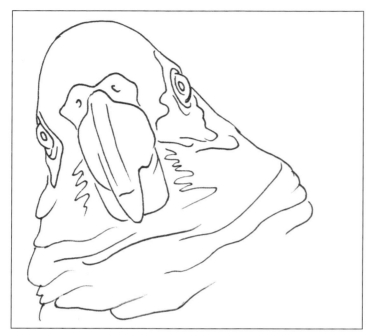

Step 1

When using colored pencils, I always transfer my drawing to a smooth sheet of drawing paper. Erased lines can leave indentations that create unwanted marks when you apply color.

Step 2

I start by applying sunburst yellow around the eyes and beak, lightening the pencil outline with an eraser as I go. Then I fill in the pupils and other areas of the eyes with warm gray 90%, being sure to leave circular highlights in each eye. I apply this same color all over the beak, varying the pressure and leaving some areas white to suggest the overall shape. Using warm gray 90% and vertical strokes, I fill in the feathers above and on the sides of the beak, as well as some random feathers on the neck and chest.

Step 3

I fill in the irises with pumpkin orange. Then I apply limepeel to most of the feathers and deepen the beak with black.

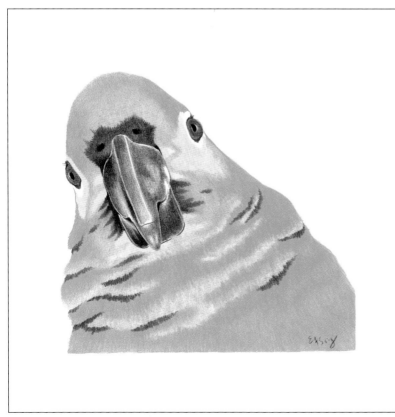

Step 4

To finish, I fill in the rest of the feathers with parrot green (how fitting!), overlapping the limepeel in places. I continue applying parrot green past my original outline, elongating the chest a bit. Then I fill in the highlights in the pupils and the holes above the beak with black.

Arabian Portrait

with Patricia Getha

Combining References

Two photo references were used for this drawing. I prefer the angle of the head and composition in the photo at left, but the horse is out of focus. I used the reference at right to compensate for this, as the details in this photo appear much sharper.

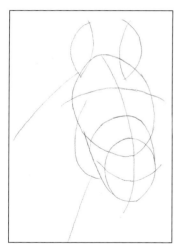

Step One

I begin this portrait with ovals for the head and muzzle; then I add several guidelines, as shown, to create reference points for adding the facial features. For example, the uppermost horizontal curve indicates the position of the top of the eyes. Now I add two lines indicating the neck and a curved line for the jaw. Then I carefully place the basic shapes of the ears.

Step Two

I add a final guideline to the left side of the horse's face for the "dish" of the muzzle (the scoop from the nostrils to the bottom of the eye, which is characteristic of Arabians). Following the guidelines, I outline and add a few details to the facial features. Then I use quick, loose strokes to begin blocking in the mane and forelock, drawing the hair in the direction of growth.

Step Three

I erase the lines I no longer need and refresh my outlines. (In this step, you may find that the guidelines aren't erasing well enough from the paper's surface. If this is the case, you can transfer your outline to a fresh sheet of paper. See step one on page 10.) I continue developing the outline, indicating the subtle changes in form over the face and neck.

Step Four

Now I switch to a 3B pencil and begin applying tone to the horse. I hatch in the shadows of the ears, face, and neck, stroking along the curves to suggest form. I use loose strokes, as I will blend them later to provide a smooth coat texture. I gradually build up the value of the forelock with long, light strokes, leaving gaps for areas of highlight.

Step Five

With the basic tonal pattern in place, I develop the shading to darken the overall value of the horse. I use a tortillon to soften and blend the layers of strokes for a more even, unified tone. I build up the mane with strokes of varying values to give it a realistic hair texture.

Step Six

In this final stage, I focus on bringing the values to their full intensity. I switch to a 6B to produce a soft, dark tone that blends easily, focusing on the areas in shadow. Once the darkest values are accurate according to the reference, I use a kneaded eraser to pull out or strengthen any highlights. For highlights in the mane, I form a kneaded eraser into a point and stroke over the mane in the direction of hair growth.

Dalmatian

with Nolon Stacey

I begin by sketching the general shape of the Dalmatian's head using an HB pencil. As this is a relatively simple head shot, I can sketch the outline without needing to block in shapes or use a grid. I make sure to capture the tilt of the head, which gives this dog great character. I ensure that the tops of the ears, eyes, and line of the mouth are all parallel and follow this tilt. I also roughly mark in some of the spots.

Step Two

Once I am happy with my outline, I begin blocking in the darkest areas using a 2B pencil. Although there are many black spots on this dog, I do not want to block in each black patch entirely, as areas of the coat still reflect light. In addition to the spots, I block in the pupil, the dark outline of the eyes, and the nostrils.

16

Step Three

I now move on to the nose and eyes. I shade the eyes using an HB pencil and radial lines around the pupil. I apply less pressure to the outer edge of the iris to give the eyes a three-dimensional quality. Then I use a blunt 2B pencil to shade the nose area, avoiding the highlights around the nostrils and on the tip. I also darken the ridge in the middle of the nose and the area beneath the nostrils.

Step Four

At this stage, I want to develop the character in the eyes, so I move on to the surrounding dark hair. I use a sharp 2B pencil to draw short lines spiraling away from the eyes. I reduce the pressure below and above the eyes (along the eyelids) to imply the eyelashes and curvature of the skin. I also mark some of the spots on the face, stroking in the direction of hair growth.

Step Five

Now I complete the black spots by adding the areas in reflected light. Again using a sharp 2B pencil, I draw short lines with the white of the paper showing through to create a lighter tone. I study my reference photo and ensure that my lines follow the direction of hair growth. To avoid a harsh line around the bottom of the drawing, I greatly lighten my pressure as I approach the bottom edge, fading out the tone.

Step Six

I now begin adding tone and texture to the white fur of the Dalmatian, which I accomplish in two stages (steps six and seven). First I apply a layer of 2H pencil over the entire neck and shoulders of the dog, again gradually fading out at the bottom of the drawing. I also use the 2H to create the cast shadow of the ear. Even as I block shade, I ensure that I stroke in the direction of hair growth. Any natural variations in the pencil strokes that occur only enhance the natural look of the hair. I use the same 2H to begin adding tone to the mouth, applying heavier pressure to the edges of the lips to create curvature. Then I add another spot to the dog's cheek.

Step Seven

I go back over the areas I have just shaded with a sharp pencil eraser. I apply strokes in the direction of the hair growth to bring out the lightest hairs. Slightly varying the shape, curvature, and direction of the strokes in areas will create a sense of depth and give a more natural look to the hair. I repeat this process on the ears and begin shading the cheeks.

Step Eight

Now I work on the white fur of the face. Because the fur is white, I don't need to worry too much about detail—only rough shading is required, as any detail would be lost in this light tone. Using the blunt side of a 2H pencil, I follow the direction of hair growth and shade below the eye and down the side of the muzzle. I also add the subtle ridge on the forehead and shade along the back of the head, where less light is hitting the coat. Then I lightly shade the area above the nose and around the mouth. The whisker markings are quite subtle, so I suggest them simply using dots and an H pencil. Finally, I return with the 2H to shade between the markings, implying separation of hair in this area.

Cat Portrait

with Nolon Stacey

Step One

I want this portrait to be very detailed and accurate, so I use the grid method to create my initial outline drawing. I begin by drawing a one-centimeter grid on a printout of my reference image (I don't want to damage the original photo).

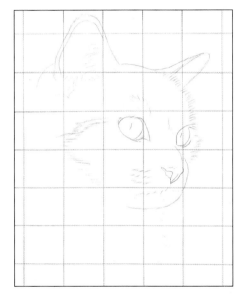

Step Two

Then I lightly draw a three-centimeter grid on my drawing paper using a 2B pencil (harder pencils can indent the paper and show through on the finished piece). This will enlarge the reference photo to three times the original size. Once I have my grid in place, I simply work through each square, transferring as much detail as I can from the reference to my paper.

Step Three

Now I completely erase any traces of my grid and redraw any parts of my line drawing that have been erased in the process. Some people prefer to erase their grid as they progress, but I prefer to start with a line drawing that is as clean as possible. I do not want to be distracted by squares during the shading process.

Step Four

As I often do, I begin by picking out the darkest areas (the nostrils and eyes) using a 2B. Notice that the pupils aren't the usual "cat" shape; because the cat's head is turned from the viewer, they appear almost as lines. To complete the iris, I use an HB pencil to fill in the eyeball with a midtone, leaving the highlights white. I then create radial lines emanating from the pupil. For the nose, I simply fill in the shape using an HB pencil, darkening slightly as I move toward the bottom.

Step Five

With the eyes and nose complete, I look at the expanse of white paper in front of me and feel quite intimidated. To break up the drawing into more manageable sections, I create some solid breaks within the fur on the head, beginning with the dark "C" shape across the cheek. For this I use a 2B pencil, first pressing quite hard to create some very dark gaps in the hair and then lightening the pressure for slightly lighter fur. I also add shading above the cat's right eye, at the base of the ear, and at the back of the head. Switching to an HB pencil, I use short lines to add the fur under the eye and up to the "C."

Step Six

I apply a layer of HB graphite over the cheek area to blend the strokes, softening the darks and eliminating the white of the paper showing through. I work my way down with the H pencil to indicate the line of the mouth, stroking in the direction of hair growth. I use a 2B pencil for the darker hairs of the mouth as well as the whisker markings. Then I layer short strokes of an HB pencil over the mouth. (I don't concern myself with whiskers yet—I will erase them at the end.) Using my 2B pencil, I create tiny "V" shapes over the forehead; the white showing through gives the impression of tapering hairs.

Step Seven

I finish the rest of the fur on the head using the same method as I used on the cheek. The hair is quite contrasting with lots of very dark areas mixed in with lighter hair. As I move toward the back of the head with the 2B pencil, I don't concern myself with detail. I want this area to appear out of focus, directing the viewer back to the face of the cat. Then I indent the long hairs in front of the insides of the ears; this will save me from having to draw around the hairs when I shade these areas.

Step Eight

I fill in the inside of each ear using an HB pencil. The impressed hairs remain free of tone. Now I get the collar in place before moving on to the chest. Whenever a collar is present in a reference photo, I like to include it. I find that it adds interest and can personalize a drawing. I shade what little of the collar is showing using a 2B pencil, drawing up into the hair laying over it. I draw the dark shadows of the metal tag using a 2B pencil and shade the smooth, shiny surface with a 2H pencil, blending it with tissue. I simply write the cat's name, Mister, with a sharp H pencil, leaving white edges to give it an engraved appearance. Then, using the H pencil, I lay down a light shadow pattern on the white hair of the cat's chest.

Step Nine

I finish the rest of the chest in two stages. First I lay down the darker areas created by partings in the hair. Then I indent some stray hairs to save time and ensure that all the white won't become covered with graphite. I want the drawing to fade out toward the bottom, so I don't include much detail along the edges; I simply block shade with an H pencil. Finally, I block shade the entire chest using a blunt HB pencil, and I blend the graphite using tissue to fade out the tone along the bottom. To bring a little detail to the area, I use a sharp vinyl eraser to cut in some lighter hairs. To complete the drawing, I add whiskers using an electric eraser, curving each one out in a single stroke from the whisker markings on the cheek. For the whiskers at left, I use curving strokes and an H pencil.

Basset Hound

with Nolon Stacey

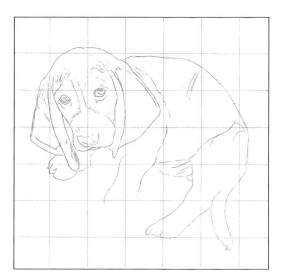

Step 1

I want to match the posture and expression of the pup as closely as possible, so I use the grid method to transfer the image to my drawing surface. I use an HB pencil to create a light grid made up of small boxes to ensure accuracy (see page 20). I also block in lines for the highlights and shadows, which will help me shade in later steps.

Step 2

Before erasing the guidelines, I make sure that I have copied over the exact shape of the puppy's eyes, as they are essential to communicating the dog's sweet, gentle expression. Then I erase the grid lines, being careful not to lose any of the dog's outline. I make sure no other adjustments are needed before progressing to the shading stage.

"Grounding" a Subject with Shadow

When rendering a full-body portrait from an unusual viewpoint, it's a good idea to "ground" the subject with a shadow. This prevents the dog from appearing to float above the drawing surface and also gives the viewer a better sense of the dog's form.

Step 3

Now I use a 2B pencil to block in the pup's right pupil, working around the highlight. I fill in the iris with a medium-dark value and create a darker outer ring, smoothing these tones with a blending stump. I darken the undereye area and begin developing the hair over the brow with short strokes.

Step 4

The skin of the brow is wrinkled. To express this, I create highlights along the tops of the folds by leaving the areas free of graphite. For the shadowed creases, I apply short strokes that are heavy and close to one another. As always, I make sure each stroke follows the direction of hair growth.

Step 5
Next I create the darkest areas on the ear using short, vertical hatching strokes. Then I apply a solid medium value of shading over the front flap of the ear, smoothing it with a tissue wrapped around my finger.

Step 6
I apply another layer of graphite over the ear (except the front flap) and blend with a tissue. I add hair over the left side of the puppy's head, stroking up and away from the eye and avoiding the white marking down the center of the head.

Now I use a 2B pencil to shade around the pup's left eye. I place the iris and pupil high in the top outer corner of the eye, with more white showing in the inner corner. This emphasizes the submissive expression. To give the eye roundness, I lightly shade the inner corner of the eye, graduating to white around the outer edge of the iris. I draw the hair below the eye, gradually fading out as the hair becomes lighter.

Step 8

Still using a 2B pencil, I begin the nose by shading the darkest areas: the underside, the nostrils, and the side. I provide texture to the top using small dark circles, gradually increasing the gaps between the circles as I approach the highlight. I complete the nose by adding midtones over the circles around the front and a very light tone to the top. I finish the muzzle with very light H pencil strokes, and I indent the whiskers with a blunt tool.

Step 9

Now I use the same method that I used in step 6 to add tone to the puppy's left ear. When I shade over the whisker indentations, they become visible.

Step 10

With an HB pencil, I accentuate the fold of the pup's left ear by giving it a very light edge to contrast with the darker hair behind it. Then I add tone to the dog's right paw, shading in between the toes. Now I'm ready to begin the back and side of the body. I again draw a series of lines in the direction of hair growth, always drawing from dark to light. I create the ridges of hair near the middle of the body by alternating light and dark values in a bumpy, striped pattern.

Step 11

I use an HB pencil to block in the rest of the hair on the back, leaving the white stripe very lightly shaded and the top of the back and the top of the left hind leg unshaded.

Step 12

With an H pencil, I add a shadow to the inner side of the hind leg and complete it and the left foreleg. I shade the stomach and blend with tissue paper to convey its nearly hairless surface. I leave the tip of the tail predominantly white.

Guinea Pig

with Eileen Sorg

Step 1

I transfer my line drawing to a clean sheet of drawing paper, and grab my colored pencils to capture the fun textures and colors of this fluffy guinea pig.

Step 2

I start laying down the fur with mineral orange, following the direction of hair growth.

Step 3

I apply blush pink to the nose, and I indicate the nostrils and mouth with hot pink. I also use blush pink on the feet and areas of the ears.

Step 4

I create darker areas of fur with burnt ochre; I also apply this color to the edges of the ears and on the feet. I fill in lighter fur areas with sand.

Step 5

I add dark shadows and fill in the eyes with espresso, leaving a highlight in each eye.

Step 6

I apply cool gray 30% and blue violet lake to create shadows in the white fur. I also use blue violet lake on the nostrils and crease below the nose. Finally, I deepen the outlines around the eyes and the shadows beneath the feet with black.

Cats in a Bag

with Nolon Stacey

Step One

With so much of the cats' bodies obscured by the bag, this is a relatively simple drawing. I don't have to worry much about the accuracy of their bodies, so I create the outline freehand. I draw the bag, and then I place the facial features and indicate the main areas of fur. I include plenty of detail in the outline, which saves me from having to assess the placement of elements as I progress. I even indicate the serrated edge of the bag.

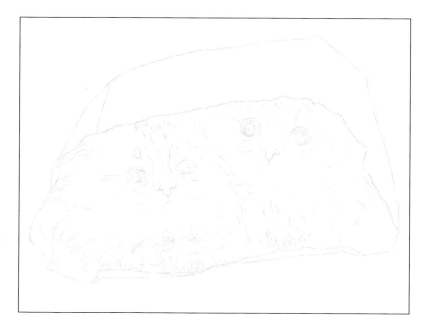

Step Two

I indent the cat's whiskers with a blunt object before shading to preserve the white of the paper. Then I begin picking out all the black areas of the drawing, blocking them in with a 2B pencil. This involves some negative drawing, which simply means that I shade around the clumps of hair. The fact that I sketched these hairs as part of the line drawing makes this process much simpler.

Step Three

I now block in the main shading of the bag using a blunt HB pencil. As I apply tone to the bag, I leave the outer edge white to help create the illusion of contrast between the cats and the bag. To model the folds and crinkles on the bag, I lift out the raised areas with an eraser and darken areas of shadow across the surface. I also add a cast shadow under the bag using the HB pencil.

Step Four

Now I address the hair on the cat at left. Beginning with the markings on the forehead, I use 2B and HB pencils to create the darker and lighter hairs, respectively. Stroking in the direction of hair growth, I move upward in the middle of the head and curve outward as I move toward the sides. Using fairly random lines, I flick some hairs off course for realism. As I get closer to the bag where the hair is in shadow, I am conscious to darken my strokes. Using this same shading method, I move across the rest of the cat's face and down onto its paws. I've already negatively drawn the darks around the paws, so I simply block in this lower area using an HB pencil. I then go over it again with a 2B pencil to add texture and create clumps of hair. I also block in the iris using an HB pencil.

33

Step Five

I finish the first cat by using an H pencil to draw fairly light lines within the fur, adding texture to the white area of the face. I also darken the area where the top lip overlaps the bottom, and I apply small circles over the nose for texture. I apply more pressure to the pencil at the sides of the nose and toward the bottom to create form. I also add the dark whisker markings on the cheeks.

Step Six

I use the exact same process to shade the next cat. I want the cat at right to be slightly lighter than the cat at left, so I leave more white paper showing through my pencil lines as I progress. I constantly turn to my reference image so I can accurately re-create the markings in my drawing, changing from the HB to the 2B pencil for the darker markings.

Step Seven

I use *block shading* (applying an even layer of graphite over an area) on the bottom half of the second cat using an HB pencil and begin to create gaps between clumps of hair using a 2B pencil. These are lines that I apply fairly randomly to change the direction of hair growth. Finally, I stroke over these clumps of hair using a sharp eraser to lighten them slightly. I also define the hairs of the cat's chin using the same eraser. To complete the drawing, I use an electric eraser to further define some of the whiskers.

Pair of Dachshunds

with Nolon Stacey

Step One

When drawing two similar dogs, like these two Dachshunds, it is important to identify and translate the differences between them. You don't want to end up with a drawing of two dogs that look identical. With this in mind, I work on both dogs simultaneously. I begin by marking out the general shape of the dogs using circles to represent the bodies and heads. Then I add rough shapes for the muzzles, ears, and legs. I want the two dogs to be looking at the same thing, but again I don't want them to look like the same image duplicated, so I slightly lower the muzzle of the dog on the right. Different positioning of the ears also helps distinguish the two.

Step Two

I now fine-tune my outline to provide a better idea of the dogs' structures. First I erase all the internal lines that aren't required, leaving just the outline of the dogs. Then I add the facial features and identify the main markings of the coats. I don't want any harsh lines that may show through later, so I use a putty eraser to lighten my line drawing until I can hardly see it. I then use it as my basis for creating a much more detailed line drawing. I mark out the main areas of hair using lines in the direction of growth. The chest is quite complex in terms of how the direction of hair growth changes, so I carefully refer to my photo reference for guidance.

Step Three

Now I block in the darkest areas of the dogs using a 2B pencil. I begin with the blacks of the nostrils and the eyes, leaving the highlights free of tone. Then I section off the areas of dark hair by simply indicating the edges with strokes that follow the direction of hair growth. I then fill in these areas with a 2B pencil, still stroking in the direction of hair growth and tapering each stroke as it moves toward the edge of the section. In this stage, I ignore any areas that do not appear black.

Step Four

Now I begin blocking in some of the larger areas of fur. I accomplish this in two stages (steps four and five). Using a 2B pencil, I apply fairly short and very dark lines over the tops of the heads, across the muzzles, and down the necks. I place the lines closer together in darker areas, such as the below the eyes, and farther apart in lighter areas, such as the tops of the heads. At this point, the white of the paper still shows between the lines, so it looks too harsh.

Step Five

The second stage involves applying a fairly dark layer of graphite over the lines to soften the look of the coats. As this is black hair, I stick with the 2B pencil to achieve a dark layer, but I am careful not to apply too much pressure—I still want the lines from steps three and four to show through. As I apply these layers, I avoid the two "brown" spots on the sides of the faces and the lighter hair behind the eyes. Then I switch to an HB and apply a lighter layer of graphite over these areas.

Step Six

I repeat this two-stage process of applying dark lines followed by a layer of shading across the necks and shoulders. Then I apply sparse guidelines in the direction of hair growth to the chests with a 2B. With hair that grows in different directions, it's important to roughly map out the flow of the hair to avoid creating unnatural-looking patches. There are essentially three crowns on the chest from which the hairs spread: one in the middle of the chest and two above the legs. The hair spirals from these crowns up to the neck and down to the stomach.

Step Seven

With these hair-growth guidelines in place, I am now confident that I can accurately add the dark lines of the chests. I do this using a 2B pencil and tapered strokes. The lines all originate from the crowns of the hair and blend into the existing strokes. You can see that this has provided the shape and structure of the chests—even without shading.

Step Eight

The lower legs and paws are brown—not black—so I layer them with an HB pencil. I use the same pencil to apply strokes over the muzzles and jaws. I start near the tops of the muzzles and lighten the pressure as I move down over the lighter cheeks. I draw the dark whisker markings, darken the shadows between the lips, and add a crease where the skin stretches to the side just below the mouth. I add whiskers with long, curved strokes. Finally, I use a 2B pencil to ground the two floating Dachshunds with simple cast shadows beneath them.

Calico Cat

with Marilyn Grame

Step 1

The basis of this drawing is a triangle. Notice the numerous angles that are apparent here. In this case I do not "round out" between them. As this calico cat is so furry, guidelines are all that are needed.

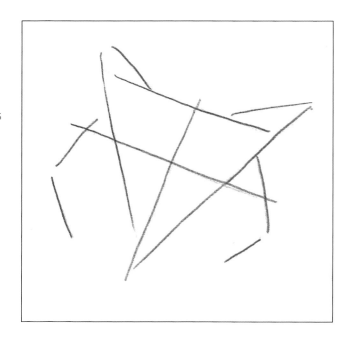

Step 2

Here I apply the distinct colors separately. I use burnt sienna and yellow ochre in varying degrees of light and dark for the warms. For a little more bright color here and there, I add some burnt sienna and a little crimson red mixed together.

Step 3

After the warms are dry, I start the darks with a cool ultramarine blue and burnt sienna mixture. I occasionally work in some heavily pigmented warm darks using ivory black with a little crimson red.

Step 4

I paint the nose with crimson red and yellow ochre. Then I add burnt sienna to the darks. I start the lovely green eyes with lemon yellow and just a touch of permanent green. I keep blending in the green, a little deeper each time, and allow the paint to dry between applications. I add a bit of diluted ivory black in the shadows and fill in the vertically elongated pupils. I emphasize the ear tufts and whiskers by lifting out color using the round brush dampened with clean water. Then I blot these areas with a tissue.

Macaw

with Marilyn Grame

Planning the Painting

With opaque media like oil and acrylic, you can change the painting at any time by adding new layers of paint. But because watercolor is more transparent, your underlying colors will show through subsequent layers of paint. Therefore, your paintings need to be well thought out before the color is applied—and an accurate sketch is essential. I first draw my subject on tracing paper and then carefully trace over the lines on the back of the paper with pencil. To transfer the drawing to my support, I tape the paper to the watercolor paper, pencil-side down, and use a coin to rub over the image. Then I remove any excess graphite from my painting support by patting it gently with a kneaded eraser.

Step One

I always begin with the background color, painting up to the edge of the main subject. If I get a little of the background wash on the bird, I know I will be able to cover it with the stronger colors and glazes I will use on the feathers. If I save the background for last, any accidental overlap on the parrot would be glaringly apparent. So to start, I wet the entire background area (including the leaves) with clean water; then I apply a graded wash of ultramarine blue with the flat brush. I add more water to each new horizontal stroke as I work downward, so the color lightens as I go. While the surface is still damp (the paint should still look shiny), I sprinkle on some salt to create a mottled texture. Then I let the paint dry completely and gently brush away the salt.

Step Two

Still using the flat brush, I begin my underpainting (my first layer of color) by working in a few different values of yellow ochre on the tree. I also glaze a layer of yellow ochre over the lighter leaves. Then I switch to the round brush to paint the majority of the macaw. I use lemon yellow to block in the neck, yellow tail feathers, and the two accent areas on the body. Next I paint a very diluted permanent green with a touch of lemon yellow on the front of the head.

Step Three

Now I use a watery ultramarine blue for the feathers on top of the head and a diluted mixture of ultramarine blue and a touch of lemon yellow for the body and tail feathers. I continue developing the form of the branches with a mixture of burnt sienna and yellow ochre, making sure my brushstrokes follow the grain of the wood. I also layer glazes of this mixture to create the darkest values of the shadows. Finally I glaze over the remaining leaves with lemon yellow.

Step Four

To add texture to the lighter leaves, I dab on some diluted permanent green with a touch of ivory black. I build up the darks under the body and tail feathers with ultramarine blue, and I add a darker value of ultramarine blue for a little variation in the feathers on the head. Then I fill in the eye with lemon yellow plus a touch of yellow ochre.

Step Five

Now I define the dark values and highlights. I begin with the macaw's head, dabbing ultramarine blue among the head feathers and outlining the green area with permanent green plus yellow ochre. I define the darker values and details of the branches with a warm mix of burnt sienna and ultramarine blue. For the leaves, I mix a cooler shade of burnt sienna and ultramarine blue and use it to create two values of grayed green—one with permanent green, the other with a mix of ultramarine blue and lemon yellow. I work from light to dark, detailing the leaves with these grayed glazes and leaving lines of the yellow underpainting to indicate the veins of the leaves. To create their rounded shapes, I dampen each leaf's edges, lightening the areas where the light hits most directly. As I paint, I keep in mind that my light source is overhead and to the left, so the highlights should fall on the top of my subject and cast shadows from the bird onto the tree branch.

Step Six

I paint the veins on the lighter leaves with a grayed permanent green, and I define the darker leaves with permanent green and yellow ochre with a touch of ivory black. Then I use yellow ochre mixed with a touch of crimson red to glaze the leaf veins and shadows, and, when dry, glaze the leaves again with ultramarine blue. Next I shape the yellow feathers, beginning with lemon yellow, then a touch of crimson red, and finally adding a touch of burnt sienna. I deepen the green feathers on the head with a progression of permanent green and a mix of permanent green and black. Then I use ultramarine blue to detail the body, using a strong wash of ultramarine blue for the darks. For the accents on the body, I mix ultramarine blue and black. I add detail to the eye and face with a mix of ultramarine blue and burnt sienna. Wrinkles are a light value of yellow ochre and crimson red.

45

Golden Retriever

with Marilyn Grame

Painting an Active Subject

Dogs are one of my favorite subjects to paint, but convincing a golden retriever like Flyer to sit still and model for an entire painting session would have been impossible. Instead I worked from a photograph. If you take your own photos, I recommend that you experiment first with different poses and film speeds until you find a shot you're pleased with and that shows the animal's personality. Then use the photo as a reference to create a realistic portrait of your furry friend.

Step One

I begin by drawing a fairly detailed sketch, indicating the areas where the colors and values change and the direction in which the fur grows. I pay careful attention to the features that make Flyer unique from other golden retrievers, such as the light areas of his face, the way his fur curls, and the shape of his eyes. But I also want to make sure I include elements of his personality: the gentle expression and the happy "grin." Then I dampen the background area and use the round brush to cover it with an ultramarine blue wash; this will provide a nice complement to the warm, golden color I'll use for his coat. I use the tip of my brush to paint around the edges of the drawing, but you may want to save the white of the paper by using liquid frisket instead. (Let it dry before painting the background, and remove it before going on to step two.)

Now I wash over the entire dog, including the eyes, nose, and tongue, with a light value of yellow ochre. This yellow ochre underpainting—or the initial layer of color—will continue to shine through subsequent layers of color and affect the way each color is perceived. It will be especially important for toning down the pink color of the tongue as the painting develops.

Step Three

Next I establish shadows and variations in the coat to give the impression of dimension and form with a darker value of yellow ochre. I build up several coats of the same dark values, letting the paint dry between each application.

Step Four

Now I paint in the red tones of the coat with the round brush, using a mixture of yellow ochre, a touch of crimson red, and a bit of burnt sienna. I pay careful attention to where the dark and light values are in my reference photo, so I am sure to establish a true likeness of Flyer. I also make sure my strokes always follow the direction in which the hair grows. Then I apply a light glaze of crimson red over his tongue and a light neutral-gray glaze of burnt sienna and ultramarine blue over his nose and lips—carefully avoiding the tooth. I also use this gray to tint the upper lip, the muzzle area, and the shadow on the tongue.

47

Step Five

This is where I begin defining Flyer's unique features. Still using the round brush, I add darker shadows to the tongue with a mix of crimson red and ivory black. I paint the nose with an ivory black wash, working around the highlight areas, and fill in the mouth using a little darker, stronger solution of black. Then I switch to the fur around the eyes and, painting light to dark, layer in a mix of yellow ochre and burnt sienna. I build up several layers of these values, letting each layer dry before adding the next, and then I repeat the process with a mix of burnt sienna and black. I add a dark layer of burnt sienna to the eyes and use it to glaze under the lid and over the shadows of the fur.

Step Six

I pick up burnt sienna on the tip of the round brush to add more layers to the coat and create details in the shadow areas. Then I mix burnt sienna and a touch of ivory black and apply this warm brown to the left sides of the irises, along with a little burnt sienna in the lower right sides. Once the irises are dry, I darken the pupils with black, working around the highlight. I pat on several glazes of black over the nose and mouth, building up to an almost-black color. I use my round brush dampened with clean water to lift out the shine of the nose and the fine whiskers, and then I blot with a tissue. Finally I tone down the tooth with a light wash of yellow ochre, using a darker value for the shadow.

Horse Portrait

with Marilyn Grame

Step 1

First, I sketch the head and neck of the colt. I include outlines for the eye, nostril, and mouth, as well as special markings, such as the diamond shape on the forehead.

Step 2

To make the lovely chestnut color, I start with a wash of yellow ochre. I reserve the white of the paper for the blaze on the forehead and the snip on the nose.

Step 3

Next I apply a wash of burnt sienna over the dry yellow ochre. I leave some of the underpainting for the highlights, and then soften the edges with a damp brush (this takes practice).

Step 4

I use burnt sienna and ultramarine blue as the basis for the darks. To deepen darker areas, I layer successive applications of this identical color and value mixture.

Step 5

I cast a darker shadow on the front of the neck and inside the ears. I use a diluted ultramarine blue and burnt sienna (gray) wash where the nose turns into shadow and for the few hairs in the center cowlick of the blaze. I define the nostril with a three-value progression of crimson red, a bit of ultramarine blue, and burnt sienna. Next I apply a few stray hairs under the chin and on the mane. Finally I add a horizontal, cigar-shaped pupil with ivory black and sign my portrait.

Pekingese

with Marilyn Grame

Step 1

I sketch the Pekingese's face and head. I keep my strokes loose, using broken lines and curves to suggest hair growth.

Step 2

First, I apply a light tan wash of yellow ochre and burnt sienna, leaving white in the eyes and around the muzzle.

Step 3

I drop a darker value of the same color mixture into the wash while it is still damp (this will allow it to blend).

Step 4
I apply a light value gray wash of burnt sienna and ultramarine blue over the muzzle and nose areas, darkening the values as the paint dries.

Step 5
I darken the ear tips and define the shadows around the muzzle and nose. For the eyes, I create three values of browns using burnt sienna and ultramarine blue. I use the deepest value for the shadows cast by the eyelids, the mid-value for local color, and the lightest value for the glows along the bottom arcs. As a finishing touch, I create a background tint of ultramarine blue to complement his warm fur.

German Shepherd

with Marilyn Grame

Step 1

I begin with a sketch of the German Shepherd, outlining the eyes, nose, and tongue. I loosely indicate divisions between areas with sharp value contrasts, such as the widows peak and around the neck.

Step 2

I create the initial wash with pale burnt sienna. I modulate values here, leaving the lightest areas above the eyes, down the left side of the face, and under the chin. When dry, I add a wash of lemon yellow and burnt sienna.

Step 3

I apply pure burnt sienna next, softening some edges and leaving others hard. This is the base coat for the darks.

Step 4

I begin applying dark values (ultramarine blue and burnt sienna) in varying degrees of warm and cool. I add more yellow ochre here and there to spice up the lights and put some crimson red in the ears. For the eyes, I work yellow ochre into burnt sienna and ultramarine blue. I try to leave some lighter areas on the nose. I paint the tongue using three values of yellow ochre and crimson red, with a bit of burnt sienna and ultramarine blue to darken. As a finishing touch, I pick out some light hairs with a damp brush, and then blot the area with a tissue.

Tropical Bird

with Marilyn Grame

Step 1

This Lilac-crowned Amazon is a bit of a challenge to paint with watercolor, as each color must be done separately and allowed to dry before proceeding to the next. However, the use of salt creates feather textures without a lot of intricate painting. I have indicated the areas where salt should be applied in red.

Step 2

I paint the green areas with permanent green and lemon yellow. While it is still wet, I add darker values using permanent green and ivory black. For more texture, I sprinkle salt on the wet paint and brush it off after the paint has dried completely.

Step 3

I apply a pale ultramarine blue with a touch of crimson red to make lavender on the top of the head, around the eye, and at the nape. Then I sprinkle salt on the top of the head, as in step two.

Step 4

I apply a wash of crimson red to the frontal plane. I gradually darken the area with more crimson red and add ivory black to the darkest parts.

Step 5

Next I work the eyes and nostrils with yellow ochre and burnt sienna. I paint the pupils ivory black and create the beak's base coat using a peachy mix of yellow ochre and burnt sienna with a touch of crimson red. Then I lay in shadows with a light mix of ultramarine blue and just a touch of ivory black. Finally I fill in the mouth with crimson red, ultramarine blue, and burnt sienna.

Horse in Action

with Marilyn Grame

Working with Photographs

I couldn't believe my luck when I was able to photograph this colt in the midst of a quick, tight turn. Here the speed of the colt's movement caused my digital image to blur a bit, but the horse's form and definition are still clear enough to make the photo useful. To add more life and vibrancy to my painting, I substituted a blue sky for the background to complement the colt's golden coat.

Step One

I lightly sketch in my composition before I begin painting, being careful to capture the correct angle of the horse's body and the movement of the forelock, mane, and tail. Then I wash clear water over the sky area. The paper absorbs the first coat of water, so I apply a second layer of water to ensure that my paint flows smoothly. Painting wet-into-wet, I apply a wash of ultramarine blue using the flat brush. I stroke in the color at an angle, leaving white spaces to simulate wispy clouds. Notice that I angled the clouds to the right, to counterbalance the thrust of the left-leaning colt.

Step Two

After the sky has dried, I block in the landscape. I wet the ground, tree, and mountain areas with clear water, but I merely dampen the edges around the dust cloud so I have more control over the flow of paint. Then I wash a light value of yellow ochre over the landscape, bringing the wash only to the damp outline of the dust cloud so that only a little color spreads along the edges. While the paint is still wet, I use a tissue to lightly blot the edges of the dust cloud to soften any hard edges.

Step Three

I define the landscape by using a diluted mix of yellow ochre and crimson red for the middle values on the mountains. When the first coat is dry, I add burnt sienna and a touch of ultramarine blue for the shadows. I build up the ground with a series of fairly light glazes: first yellow ochre and then burnt sienna. Next I tone permanent green with some ivory black and paint the trees and ground cover. I keep this subtle so it doesn't vie with the subject.

Step Four

When the background is dry, I wash yellow ochre over the colt, painting around the white mane, tail, blaze, and stockings. I continue to work on the ground detail, using the same grayed permanent green washes and yellow ochre and burnt sienna from step three to build up the dark areas in the dry dirt and vegetation.

Step Five

To define my light source, I highlight the colt from the right side, and I indicate the shadows on the left. I build up the shadows using a second glaze of yellow ochre, this one with more pigment and less water. Next I begin defining the shadows in the white areas, using a light wash of ultramarine blue mixed with burnt sienna.

Step Six

Now I add my darkest values. I glaze yellow ochre and then burnt sienna over the colt, letting each glaze dry before applying the next. Then I define the shadows in the whites and darken the cast shadows with a mix of ultramarine blue and burnt sienna. I also continue refining the vegetation with the grayed permanent green mix. I lightly wash over the dust cloud with the ultramarine blue and burnt sienna mix and pat the damp area with a tissue. Finally I add highlights at the ends of the mane and tail by scraping off paint with a utility knife.

Shetland Sheepdog

with Marilyn Grame

Step 1

I begin with an outline of the sheltie, sketching in the eyes, nose, and marking on the forehead.

Step 2

To create the reddish-brown coat, I mix yellow ochre, burnt sienna, and a touch of crimson red. I make sure to leave all the whites, because I can't get them back later!

Step 3

Next, I apply a darker, more heavily pigmented value of the same color with some ultramarine blue added.

Step 4

I paint the extreme darks "in the negative;" basically, I just paint the dark areas around light hair strands. I create shadows in the whites with delicate touches of an ultramarine blue and burnt sienna mixture. I refine the nose and the eye, leaving the white highlights. Then I pull out the fine hairs with the round brush.

Closing Words

Pets come in a delightful range of shapes, sizes, colors, textures, and personalities, offering tons of inspiring subjects for portraits. Once you become comfortable with the drawing and painting techniques demonstrated in this book, experiment with other materials and approaches to figure out your own unique style. Most of all, we hope that you have fun with all of your creative adventures capturing the likeness of your most beloved pets.